A STEP-BY-STEP BOOK

ANIMALS and THEIR YOUNG

Written by Anita Ganeri

Artwork by John Mac and John Rielly

WISHING WELL BOOKS®

CONTENTS

Published by Wishing Well Books,
an imprint of Joshua Morris Publishing, Inc.,
221 Danbury Road, Wilton, CT 06897.

Copyright © 1994 Salamander Books Limited,
129-137 York Way, London N7 9LG.
All rights reserved. Printed in Belgium.

ISBN: 0-88705-754-3

10 9 8 7 6 5 4 3 2 1

Wishing Well Books & Design is a registered trademark of
The Reader's Digest Association, Inc.

INTRODUCTION

Some animals are very caring parents. They feed and protect their young until they are old enough to leave home and look after themselves. Other parents abandon their young as soon as they are born. But even the least caring parents will often go to great lengths to make sure that their young are well supplied with fresh food in their absence.

Through step-by-step illustrations, this book explores some of the more unusual ways in which animals care for their young. It also looks at the amazing series of changes that some animals go through before becoming adults. At the end of *Animals and Their Young*, you'll find a fun quiz to test your knowledge as well as a glossary to explain some of the special terms used in the book.

LIFE CHANGES

Butterflies start life as tiny eggs. Then they go through an amazing series of changes to become adult butterflies. This set of changes is called metamorphosis.

First, the eggs hatch into caterpillars. These spend their time feeding on leaves and growing bigger. Then each caterpillar hangs upside down from a leaf or stem and spins a silk case around itself. This stage is known as a chrysalis, or pupa. Eventually, the chrysalis splits open and an adult butterfly struggles out. The adult stage is called an imago. The butterfly may live only a few weeks and in that time must find a mate and produce its own eggs.

1

In the first stage of a swallowtail butterfly's life, a female butterfly lays a single egg on a juicy leaf. Then the mother leaves her egg to look after itself.

2

After about 10 days, a brightly colored caterpillar hatches from the egg. It begins to eat its way through the surrounding leaves.

3

When the caterpillar is fully grown, it spins a silk chrysalis around itself. Inside, the caterpillar's body is completely rebuilt into an adult butterfly.

4

A few weeks later, the chrysalis splits and the adult emerges. Its wings are soft and crumpled but soon become stiff and smooth as blood flows into them.

A FOND FATHER

In nature, it is the mother who gives birth to the young. Sea horses, however, are very unusual because it looks as if the male instead of the female is giving birth.

A few days before mating, the male sea horse grows a small pocket, or pouch, on his belly. The female then squirts her eggs into the pouch and the male fertilizes them. A couple of weeks later, hundreds of tiny baby sea horses burst out of the father's pouch. It may take 24 hours for all the babies to swim free. Then he leaves the babies to look after themselves. The male sea horse flushes out his pouch with water to clean it and make it ready for the next brood. Some sea horses may have three groups of babies every year.

1

First, the male and female sea horses face each other and coil their tails together. Then the female squirts hundreds of tiny eggs into the male's pouch.

2

The eggs are fertilized inside the male's pouch and begin to grow into tiny baby sea horses. They feed on a special liquid made inside the pouch.

3

About two weeks later, the male curls his tail around some seaweed and begins to rock back and forth. Suddenly, a mass of tiny sea horses starts to shoot out of his pouch.

4

The baby sea horses swim free and head straight for the surface. There they take in air to fill their swim bladders. This helps them to stay upright in the water.

POCKET NURSERY

Kangaroos belong to a group of animals called marsupials. The females of this group have deep pockets, or pouches, on their stomachs that they use as nurseries for their young.

A newborn baby kangaroo looks nothing like its parents. It looks like a pink, hairless grub the size of a bean. This tiny baby has to crawl up its mother's body to her pouch — a dangerous journey for such a small creature. Six months later, the young kangaroo, or joey, makes its first journey outside the pouch. It quickly hops back in if it is tired or frightened. Even when it leaves the pouch for good, after nine months, it still sticks its head inside for a drink. By this time, a tiny new baby may be drinking its mother's milk inside the pouch, and another baby may be waiting to be born.

1

A baby kangaroo is only about an inch long at birth. It is pink, blind, and helpless. Hanging on with its tiny arms, it manages to crawl through its mother's fur and up to the pouch. This journey takes about three minutes.

2

After the baby kangaroo has climbed inside its mother's pouch, it attaches itself to one of her nipples. The baby starts to drink its mother's milk. Soon it begins to grow bigger and stronger.

10

3

As the baby grows inside the pouch, it begins to look more like a kangaroo. It develops a long tail and long back legs, and grows fur. Finally, it is old enough to venture outside.

STANDING GUARD

Insects are not usually very caring parents. They lay their eggs and leave them to hatch on their own. Their young must fend for themselves. But parent bugs are different. To protect her young from enemies such as birds, the mother stands guard over them, sheltering them with her body.

Baby bugs are called nymphs. They stay close by their mother until they are older and big enough to set off on their own.

Adult parent bugs feed on the juicy sap found inside birch leaves and stems. They pierce holes in the leaves with their sharp, beaklike jaws and suck out the sap. Parent bugs belong to a group of insects known as shield-backed bugs, earning their name from their folded wings, which look like a soldier's shield.

1 The mother bug lays her eggs on a birch leaf. She lays them in a diamond-shaped clump that is just the right size for her to cover with her body.

2 Two to three weeks later, the eggs hatch into tiny, wingless nymphs that look similar to their parents. Their mother still stands over them to protect them.

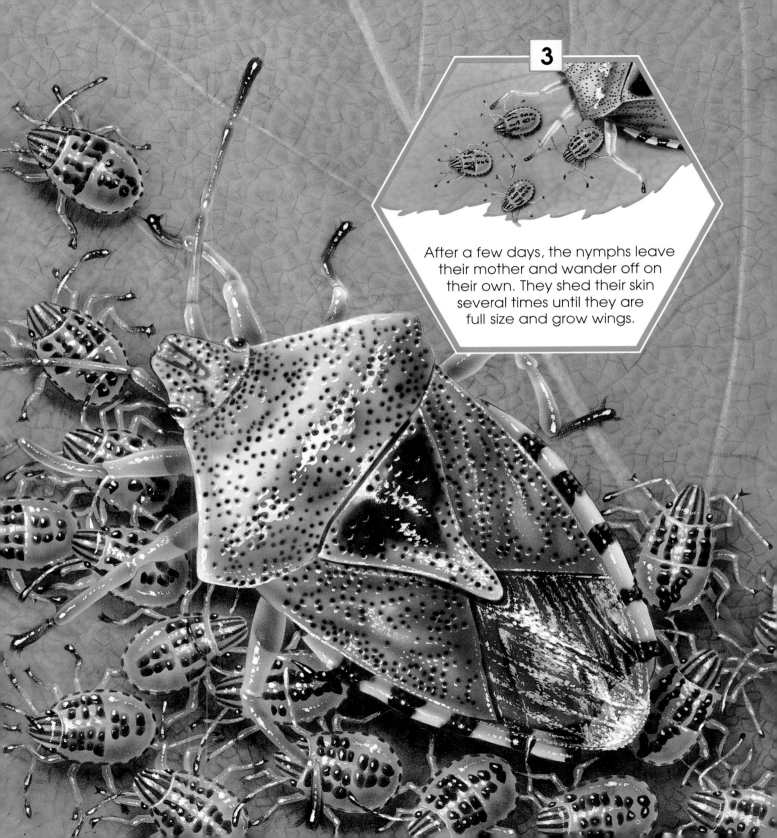

3

After a few days, the nymphs leave their mother and wander off on their own. They shed their skin several times until they are full size and grow wings.

TADPOLE TO TOAD

Toads belong to a group of animals called amphibians. These creatures live a double life. They spend the early part of their lives in water but most of their adult lives on land. Even so, they tend to stay close to the water. The reason is that they breathe through their skin as well as their lungs and they need to keep their skin damp so it can soak in oxygen.

Toads hibernate (go into a deep sleep) during the winter. When they wake up in the spring, the toads make their way back to the pond where they were born. Here they mate and lay their eggs in the water. The eggs do not hatch into baby toads. Instead, they hatch into tiny fishlike babies called tadpoles. The tadpoles gradually change into small toads over the next few weeks, until they are ready for life on land. The series of changes that a toad goes through from an egg to an adult is called metamorphosis.

1 The female toad lays long strings of eggs, or spawn, in the water. She winds the strings around waterweeds to anchor them in place. Then she leaves them for good.

2 About 10 days later, the eggs hatch into tiny legless tadpoles. Like fish, tadpoles swim using their long tails. They breathe through their feathery gills.

3

Over the next two to three months, the tadpoles turn into tiny toads. Their tails and gills disappear; they grow legs for walking and develop lungs for breathing.

4

Finally, the baby toads leave their pond for the first time to begin their adult lives on land. They shed their skin several times as they develop into fully grown adults.

CROCODILE CARE

People used to think that crocodiles ate their own babies because they saw them picking the babies up in their mouths. In fact, crocodiles are extremely caring parents. Far from eating their young, they carry them gently in their mouths down to the water for their first swim.

The female crocodile guards her babies from the time she lays her eggs until about two months after they hatch. Even then, the little crocodiles stay near their mother until they are two years old. The mother constantly listens out for their distress calls. Young crocodiles have many enemies, including hungry fish and herons. If danger threatens, the mother crocodile quickly scoops her young back up into her mouth.

1

The female crocodile lays her eggs in a hole she has dug near the water's edge. Then she covers the eggs with earth and plants to hide them from such predators as lizards and mongooses.

2

The mother sits on or near the nest for about three months, guarding her eggs until they hatch. When she hears squeaking noises coming from beneath the ground, she knows it is time to dig the eggs up.

3

The baby crocodiles use a special knob of bone on the nose, called an egg tooth, to break out of their shells. Then their mother carefully picks them up in her mouth and carries them down to the water.

SPIDERS FOR SUPPER

Spider-hunting wasps are fierce predators, able to catch spiders as big as themselves or even bigger. Some even take on tarantulas. The female wasp in the main picture here has her eyes on a large trapdoor spider. Spider-hunting wasps, however, do not hunt spiders for themselves — adult wasps only eat flower nectar. Instead, they are looking for a meal for their young.

After she has laid her single egg, the female wasp leaves her young to fend for itself. But she has a very clever way of making sure it is well fed, even in her absence. She does this by laying her egg on the body of a paralyzed spider. When the egg hatches, the larva has a good supply of spider meat to feed on. By paralyzing the spider rather than killing it, the female wasp makes sure that the meat stays fresh for her larva. Then she goes off to find a new victim on which to lay another egg.

1

The female wasp digs her burrow in the ground. Then she goes in search of a nearby spider. Avoiding its poisonous fangs, she stings the spider to paralyze it.

2

The wasp drags the spider down into her burrow. She may bite the spider's legs off to make her prey easier to move and to make extra sure it stays put.

3

The wasp lays an egg on the spider's body, then seals up the burrow entrance. When the larva hatches, it feeds on the spider meat safely inside the burrow.

19

A Mouthful!

Many fish simply lay their eggs in the water and swim away, leaving the eggs to look after themselves. A very few fish, such as sticklebacks, build underwater nests in which to raise their young. But one amazing group of fish, called mouthbrooders, has a very unusual way of looking after its young. These fish carry their eggs and babies around in their mouths.

After fertilization, the female scoops up the eggs into her mouth. The eggs remain there until they hatch. During this time the female cannot eat or swallow, no matter how hungry she may get, because she may accidentally swallow the eggs. After hatching, the baby fish continue to live inside their mother's mouth for a week or so, making short trips outside. Then they swim away for good, old enough to look after themselves.

1

The female mouthbrooder lays her eggs in the water. She may lay as many as 100 eggs in just half an hour. Then the male fish fertilizes her eggs.

2

The female scoops up the eggs into her mouth to keep them safe from their enemies. The tiny baby fish hatch after about 10 days inside their mother's mouth.

3

Soon the young fish are making short trips outside their mother's mouth. They stay close by and get back inside quickly if danger threatens.

SCORPION RIDE

Scorpions have a deadly weapon — the sting at the tip of their tails. It contains a strong poison that the scorpion injects into its prey or an attacker. The poison of some scorpions is strong enough to kill a person in less than an hour. It's not surprising that scorpions are considered to be very dangerous animals.

But scorpions have their good side, too. The mother looks after her young very carefully until they are old enough to fend for themselves. She does this by carrying them around on her back, out of reach of their enemies. If an enemy does get too close, the mother threatens it with her sting. As the baby scorpions get older and bigger, however, it becomes more uncomfortable for their mother to carry them around. After a few days, they scramble down and set off on their own.

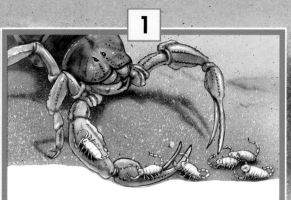

1

Scorpion eggs hatch almost at once after they have been laid. The tiny babies then climb up their mother's pincers and onto her back. They are white at this stage.

2

The baby scorpions cling to their mother's back with their tiny legs and sharp pincers. If a baby falls off, its mother stops and waits for it to climb back up again.

3

After a few days, the babies are too big or too painful to carry any longer. So they leave their mother to look after themselves. By now, they have changed to their adult color.

A Dash to the Sea

Sea turtles spend most of their lives in the water. They are perfectly suited to underwater life, with powerful flippers to help them swim. Several times a year, however, the female turtles come ashore to lay their eggs. Some swim vast distances to their nesting sites. Green turtles, for instance, swim 1,250 miles across the Atlantic Ocean from their feeding grounds in Brazil to their nesting beaches on Ascension Island. When they arrive at the nesting site, the female turtles haul themselves out of the water and onto the beach, where they dig a large nesting hole in the sand. Then they lay their eggs and return to the sea.

It's a risky business for the young. Both eggs and babies make tasty meals for birds, crabs, mammals, and humans, and turtle nests are often raided. A large number of newly hatched turtles are also caught and killed as they dash for the safety of the sea. In addition, many nesting beaches are now being destroyed by hotels and tourists. As a result, sea turtles have become very rare, and some types are close to extinction.

1

The mother sea turtle digs a hole in the sand with her back flippers. She lays about 100 round, white eggs in her nest and then covers them up with sand.

2

The baby turtles hatch from the eggs. The eggshells are quite soft, so they are easy to break out of. Next, the babies dig their way out of the sand.

3

Now begins the turtles' first and most dangerous journey. They have to scurry to the sea as quickly as possible to avoid being eaten by gulls or crabs.

FLOCK FAMILY

Swans live on slow-moving rivers and on lakes, and feed on waterweeds and grass. During the winter, they often live in large flocks, made up of smaller family units containing a mother, father, and several cygnets (young swans).

Most swans pair up for life. The parents work together to build their waterside nest out of grass and weeds. Then the female swan sits on the eggs until they hatch. Afterward, the father helps her to care for the cygnets and guides the young swans on their first winter migration (journey to warmer lands). Newly hatched cygnets look awkward and clumsy, and their plumage is a dull gray. Swans do not grow their beautiful white plumage until they are about three years old.

1

The mother swan lays her eggs in a large nest that she and her mate have built at the water's edge. She may lay up to eight eggs.

2

The mother guards her nest fiercely against enemies that get too close. She can badly injure them by flapping her powerful wings.

3

The eggs hatch after about five weeks. Although the cygnets are able to swim immediately, they will often ride on their mother's back for safety.

27

FUN QUIZ TIME

Now that you have learned how different wild animals raise their young, why not test your knowledge with this fun quiz? The questions are all based on information given in the previous pages. And just in case you can't remember an answer, we've put all the answers on page 31. Good luck!

(a) What are the four stages of a butterfly's life called?
(b) How many eggs does a swallowtail butterfly lay?
(c) What happens to the caterpillar's body inside the chrysalis?
(d) Are the new butterfly's wings stiff or soft at first?

(a) Does the mother or father sea horse have the babies?
(b) Where are sea horse eggs kept until they hatch?
(c) How many baby sea horses are born at one time?
(d) Why do the babies swim straight to the surface after they are born?

(a) A marsupial is an animal with a pouch. What is the pouch used for?
(b) What does a newborn kangaroo look like?
(c) What is a young kangaroo often called?
(d) How old is the young kangaroo when it makes its first trip outside the pouch?

(a) How does a mother parent bug protect her eggs from their enemies?
(b) The mother parent bug lays her eggs in a special shape. What shape is it?
(c) What are newly hatched parent bugs called?
(d) How have shield-backed bugs earned their name?

(a) Which group of animals do toads belong to?
(b) What are toads' eggs called?
(c) How are toads' eggs laid in the water — singly or in long strings?
(d) How do newly hatched tadpoles breathe — through their lungs or their gills?

(a) Where does a mother crocodile lay her eggs?
(b) How does a mother crocodile know when her eggs are ready to hatch?
(c) What do baby crocodiles use to break open their shells?
(d) How does a mother crocodile pick up her young?

(a) Do adult spider-hunting wasps eat spiders?
(b) What does the wasp do to the spider as soon as it has caught it?
(c) Where does the wasp lay its egg?
(d) What does the wasp larva eat after it has hatched?

(a) Where do mouthbrooders keep their young?
(b) Why can't the mother eat while she is caring for her eggs?
(c) How long does it take a mouthbrooder egg to hatch?
(d) What do the baby fish do if danger threatens when they are swimming outside?

(a) Why does the mother scorpion carry her young on her back?
(b) What color are newly hatched baby scorpions?
(c) How do the baby scorpions cling to their mother's back?
(d) What happens if a baby falls off its mother's back?

(a) Where do female turtles lay their eggs?
(b) What does the mother turtle use to dig her nesting hole?
(c) How many eggs does the mother lay at one time?
(d) Why do baby turtles dash to the sea as fast as possible after they have hatched?

(a) What are young swans called?
(b) How does the mother swan frighten away her enemies?
(c) Why do the baby swans ride on their mother's back?
(d) How old are the young swans when they turn white in color?

29

GLOSSARY

Amphibians A group of animals, including frogs and toads, that spend part of their lives in water and part on land.

Brood A family of baby animals that have hatched from the same clutch (group) of eggs.

Chrysalis The stage in a butterfly's or moth's life when the animal is enclosed in a silk case and its body changes from a caterpillar into an adult. Also, the silk case itself.

Cygnet A young swan.

Egg tooth A knob of bone on a baby bird's beak or a baby crocodile's nose that the animal uses to break open its eggshell.

Extinct An animal that no longer exists, such as a dinosaur or mammoth.

Fertilize The combination of a substance (called sperm) from a male animal and a female's egg that results in a new baby.

Flock A group of animals, such as birds, sheep, or goats, that live together.

Hibernate Go into a deep sleep during winter to save energy while food is scarce.

Imago The adult stage of an insect's life after the animal has undergone metamorphosis; for example, an adult butterfly.

Incubate Keeping an egg at the right temperature for the baby to develop properly inside. Many animals sit on their eggs to incubate them.

Joey A young kangaroo.

Larva The stage in an insect's life between egg and pupa; for example, a caterpillar.

Marsupials A group of animals that have pouches on their bellies in which they raise their young.

Metamorphosis The series of changes that insects and amphibians go through in their lives as they develop from eggs into adults.

Nectar A sweet, syrupy liquid found deep inside flowers. It is a favorite food of insects such as bees and butterflies.

Oxygen A gas found in air and water that plants and animals breathe in order to survive.

Paralyzed Unable to move. Some animals are able to paralyze other animals with their sting.

Plumage A bird's feathers.

Predator An animal that hunts and eats other animals.

Prey An animal that is hunted and eaten by other animals.

Pupa The stage in an insect's life when the animal is enclosed in a case and changes from a larva into an adult.

Sap The sugary juice that travels around inside plants.

Spawn The eggs of frogs and toads; also, to lay such eggs.

Swim bladder A long pouch inside a fish's body. A fish can fill it with air to stay upright in the water.